LEARN ABOUT

SHARKS

THE GREAT WHITE SHARK

BY MATT "THE SHARK GUY" MARCHANT

 FriesenPress

Suite 300 - 990 Fort St
Victoria, BC, V8V 3K2
Canada

www.friesenpress.com

ISBN
978-1-5255-3392-1 (Hardcover)
978-1-5255-3393-8 (Paperback)
978-1-5255-3394-5 (eBook)

1. JUVENILE NONFICTION, ANIMALS, MARINE LIFE

Distributed to the trade by The Ingram Book Company

FOR MAVERICK. DREAM BIG SON.

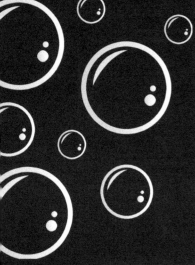

LEARNING OBJECTIVES/
CONTENTS

- How old are sharks?
- What is the scientific classification of the Great White?
- Where can we find Great White Sharks?
- How do scientists track the sharks?
- What is the anatomy of a Great White Shark?
- How do they hunt?
- How do they bite?
- How can YOU save the SHARKS?
- Plus! More cool shark facts and pictures!

MEET THE SHARK GUY:

When I was young, I only saw sharks on TV or read about them in books. They were always larger than life as they swam through my imagination. It was my dream to see these animals in the wild. I followed that dream. I have now spent hundreds of hours underwater capturing their beauty with my camera. Let your imagination run wild as you look through this book. Allow the sharks to swim through your dreams. I hope that one day you too can see these amazing creatures face to face!

–Matt

HOW OLD ARE SHARKS?

The oldest shark in the fossil record goes back over 400 million years! Sharks were swimming in the oceans for 200 million years before dinosaurs walked the earth. Using the timeline on the next page, can you name two other types of animals that came AFTER sharks?

Shark Fact

How old are Sharks?

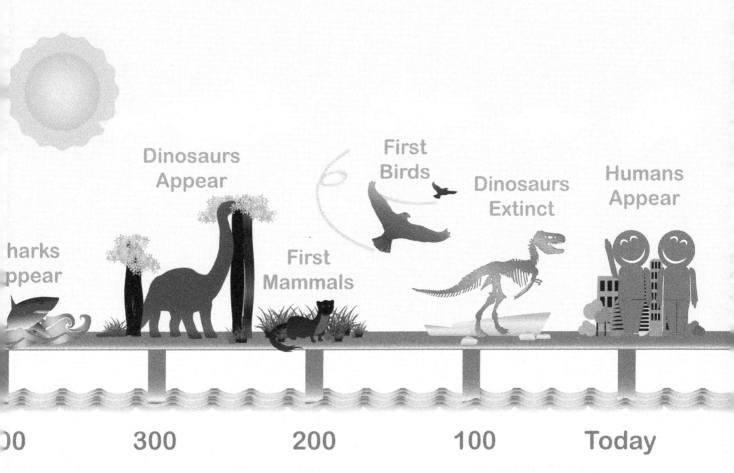

Sharks are older than the Dinosaurs!

Scientific Classification of the
Great White Shark - Carcharodon Carcharias

This is the classification tool that is used for all living organisms
Kingdom:
Animalia

The Kingdom is split into FIVE groups of Animals. Great White Sharks are
Phylum:
Chordata
vertebrates, animals with a spinal column

Within Chordata we hav- classes of animals. Sharks are
Class:
Chrondrichthye
Fish with skeletons made of cartilage

In each Class there are Orders. Sharks with five gills, two dorsal fins, an anal fin, and higher body temperatures are in
Order:
Lamniformes

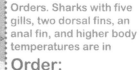

Within each order there is a Family - Great Whites ar- part of
Family:
Lamnidae
large, fast-swimming sharks with big teeth

The basic unit of classification is Species. Great White Sharks are
Species:
Carcharias
It's name means Sharp Tooth Shark (Greek Translation).

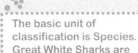

Genuses exist within each Family, The Great White is part of
Genus:
Carcharadon
It is the last surviving member

WHERE CAN WE FIND THE GREAT WHITE SHARK?

The dark blue areas on the map are locations around the world where Great Whites are commonly found. As a shark matures, their habitat range increases. They will travel many miles every year. Great White Sharks are found in every ocean on Earth.

Shark Fact

Great White Shark Global Habitat

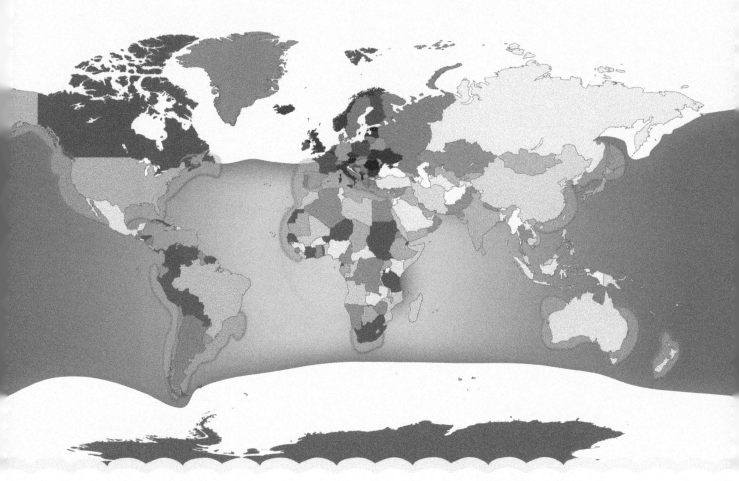

 Global Range of Great White Shark

 Coastal Habitat of Great White Shark

HOW DO SCIENTISTS TRACK THE SHARKS?

Scientists use satellite tags to record the movement of sharks. When the shark swims near the surface of the water, the location is recorded by the tag. The data helps marine biologists understand where the sharks go. Using the picture on the next page, can you find the satellite tracking tag?

Shark Fact

HOW FAR DO THEY SWIM?

In a single year, a shark may travel up to 12,000 miles (19,312 km)! The longest single Great White swim ever tracked by scientists is over 9,000 miles (14,484 km). A female Great White swam from the southern tip of Africa to Australia and back again over a nine-month period.

Shark Fact

Scientists have identified over 250 different Great Whites at Guadalupe Island, Mexico. The shark's photos are kept in a Scientific Catalogue that is updated every year.

Shark Fact

SHARK DIVING SAFETY

The safest way to see Great White Sharks is inside a shark cage. Safety is very important when diving with sharks. It is important to keep the divers and sharks safe.

Shark Fact

LEARN WHITE
SHARK ANATOMY

Use the diagram on the right to learn the anatomy of a Great White Shark. Then test your knowledge by naming all the shark's body parts in the following pictures!

Shark Fact

White Shark Anatomy

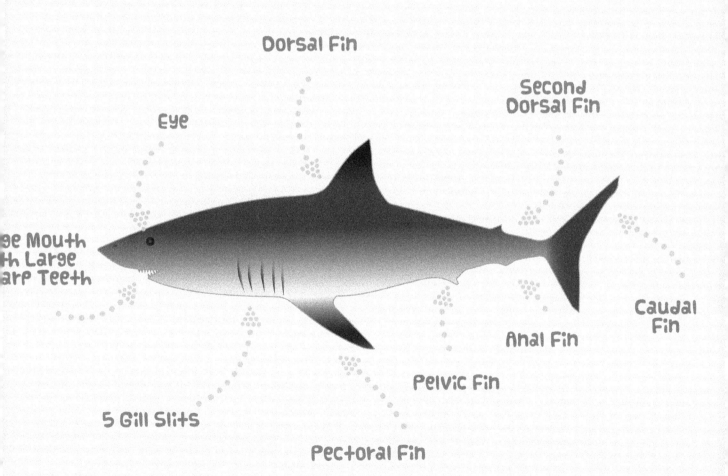

Dorsal Fin

Second
Dorsal Fin

Eye

ge Mouth
th Large
arp Teeth

Caudal
Fin

Anal Fin

5 Gill Slits

Pelvic Fin

Pectoral Fin

Ambush Predator

3. If the shark times the attack just right, then it will have a very filling meal.

1. The shark swims silently below its prey.

2. Reaching an average of 25 miles per hour, the Great White breaches the surface and leaps 8-10 feet (2-3 metres) in the air.

The Great White eats approximately 11 tons (9,979 kg) of food a year! The average human eats close to one ton (907 kg) of food a year

Shark Fact

The most memorable part of Great White Sharks are their jaws.

The jaw is made of cartilage and is filled with hundreds of teeth. During a bite, the shark lifts the nose, opens the lower jaw and thrusts the upper jaw forward and down.

The mouth closes to complete the bite. This allows the shark to make larger bites on prey.

Once a bite is complete, the jaw goes back to it's resting position.

BITE MECHANICS
of a Great White

The Great White Shark has around 300 teeth in its mouth arranged in multiple rows. Sharks lose thousands of teeth during their life. Fortunately, they are constantly growing new rows of teeth to replace those that fall out.

Shark Fact

SHARKS NEED YOUR HELP! EVERY YEAR, IT IS ESTIMATED THAT 70-100 MILLION SHARKS ARE KILLED FOR THEIR FINS. GREAT WHITE SHARKS ARE CURRENTLY CLASSIFIED AS "VULNERABLE" ON THE ENDANGERED SPECIES LIST BECAUSE OF OVERFISHING. WE MUST LEARN MORE ABOUT THESE SHARKS AND RAISE AWARENESS SO THAT THESE AMAZING ANIMALS CAN CONTINUE TO SWIM IN THE OCEANS FOR MANY GENERATIONS TO COME!

HOW CAN YOU SAVE THE SHARKS?

- Donate or volunteer with a Shark Conservation Organization.
- Teach others about sharks! Education is the key to conservation.
- Don't eat at restaurants that sell shark fin soup.
- Keep the oceans clean. Reduce, Reuse, Recycle.
- Write letters to local and national law makers asking for laws to protect sharks.
- Go see sharks in person! Most aquariums around the world have live sharks for you to see up close. These aquariums help with research and assist in saving our oceans!

GLOSSARY

ANATOMY – study of the structure or internal workings of an animal.

AMBUSH – to make a surprise attack.

CARCHARODON CARCHARIAS - Scientific name for the Great White Shark.

CARTILAGE – flexible connective tissue that makes up the shark's skeleton. You have cartilage in your ears and nose!

CONSERVATION – protecting and preserving the natural environment.

ENDANGERED SPECIES – a species of animal or plant that is at risk of extinction.

EXTINCT – an animal or plant that has no living members.

FOSSIL – the remains (usually the bones) of an animal preserved in rock. For sharks, their teeth are what become fossils over millions of years.

GPS – Global Positioning System – pinpoints where the shark is.

HABITAT – the natural environment for an animal.

MECHANICS – science of motion and forces producing motion.

PREDATOR – an animal that preys on other animals.

PREY – an animal that is hunted by another animal for food.

SATELLITE TAG – scientific tool used to track shark movement. Tags are placed at the base of the dorsal fin and record GPS information every time the shark is at the water's surface.

SCIENTIFIC CATALOGUE – a database of the sharks. Scientists use them to record all known data and information about the sharks.

SHARK CAGE – large metal box that scuba divers use to safely view sharks.

SHARK FIN SOUP – soup containing shark fins that is considered an expensive delicacy in some countries.

CPSIA information can be obtained
at www.ICGtesting.com
Printed in the USA
LVHW010754191118
597620LV00024B/924/P